THE GOLDEN AGE

A three-act ballet

"The Golden Age" nightclub—the epitome of the last days of bourgeoisie in the young Soviet Republic. The old style is having its last swing...

Published through the cooperation
of VAAP Copyright Agency of the Soviet Union.

THE GOLDEN AGE
A three-act ballet

Music by
Dmitry Shostakovich
Stage production and Choreography by

Yuri Grigorovich

Produced in 1982

Distributed in the UNITED STATES by T.F.H. Publications, Inc., One T.F.H. Plaza, Neptune City, NJ 07753; in CANADA to the Book Trade by Macmillan of Canada (A Division of Canada Publishing Corporation), 164 Commander Boulevard, Agincourt, Ontario M1S 3C7; in ENGLAND by T.F.H. Publications Limited, Cliveden House/Priors Way/Bray, Maidenhead, Berkshire SL6 2HP, England; in AUSTRALIA AND THE SOUTH PACIFIC by T.F.H. (Australia) Pty. Ltd., Box 149, Brookvale 2100 N.S.W., Australia; in NEW ZEALAND by Ross Haines & Son, Ltd., 18 Monmouth Street, Grey Lynn, Auckland 2, New Zealand; in SINGAPORE AND MALAYSIA by MPH Distributors (S) Pte., Ltd., 601 Sims Drive, #03/07/21, Singapore 1438; in the PHILIPPINES by Bio-Research, 5 Lippay Street, San Lorenzo Village, Makati Rizal; in SOUTH AFRICA by Multipet Pty. Ltd., 30 Turners Avenue, Durban 4001. Published by T.F.H. Publications, Inc. Manufactured in the United States of America by T.F.H. Publications, Inc.

THE AUTHORIZED BOLSHOI BALLET BOOK OF
THE GOLDEN AGE

By Yuri Grigorovich and Sania Davlekamova

Translated by Tim Coey
Photography by Vladimir Pchalkin
Captions to color photographs by Dr. Herbert R. Axelrod

CONTENTS

In order to understand the story of *THE GOLDEN AGE* and the meaning of the various dances and scenes, begin reading the captions to the color photographs starting on page 57. Synopsis of the ballet is on page 56.

The way Yuri Grigorovich stages Dmitry Shostakovich's ballet **The Golden Age** makes it an event of much more magnitude than a talented new show!

Nadezhda Pavlova, a young Bolshoi Ballet star, congratulating Yuri Grigorovich on his sixtieth birthday. The Bolshoi Hall, Moscow.

Yuri Grigorovich Recollects:

Fate presented me the good fortune of association with Dmitry Shosta-kovich, a great composer and great person. That gift of fate was made the more generous by his noting my very first stage productions and expressing an opinion on them in the press. You can imagine what the praise of such a personality meant for me as a 30-year-old ballet-master. And Shostakovich continued to follow my career. We got to know each other and would meet and talk . . . Our get-togethers were not all that frequent but the wisdom of the words of such an interlocutor gave me direction and determined my future creative quests. To this day all those memories remain in my heart and soul.

I naturally dreamed of working with him, of staging a ballet of his. Alas, to my deep regret, my stage production came only in 1982 and Dmitry Shostakovich did not live to see it.

"The Golden Age" was his first ballet. He composed it straight out of the Leningrad Conservatory. Just as his two other ballets, this one had a dramatic and unjust destiny of which the reader will learn in the book. Let me say that just after the first unsuccessful stage productions, Shostakovich's ballet works were forgotten for over 50 years. I'm proud that it was the Bolshoi Theater, the standard bearer of Russian culture, that initiated the return of the ballet heritage left by a fine composer. I likewise feel privileged to have played a part in restoring that Shostakovich heritage to the stage.

I find the music in "The Golden Age" stunning. It sounds as if it were written only today. It is exceptionally theatrical, brightly and effectively oper-atic, something which strangely enough is not so common in the art of ballet. Shostakovich's music draws images that seem to fill the mind's eye. And let me just note that this is jolly music with plenty of flight of fantasy which has always been the all-important thing for choreographic theater.

It was a joy and pleasure to work on the ballet. Unforgettable months, some of the best days of my life.

Dmitry Shostakovich (1907-1975)

Chapter 1

The Fate of the Shostakovich Ballets

The way Yuri Grogorovich stages the Dmitry Shostakovich ballet, "The Golden Age," makes it an event of much more magnitude than a talented new show. Here we have the triumph of truth, something important for choreography and music in general. We see a new aspect discovered in the work of a composer of world renown who is performed by the most illustrious orchestras and most eminent musicians and whose operas are performed in the world's foremost houses. Interestingly, ballets are performed in the USSR and abroad to Shostakovich music not intended for dance theater. The Shostakovich ballet heritage remained a long time unrecognized in his homeland and internationally.

Yet Shostakovich was one of the first composers to write for the emergent Soviet school of dance. Three ballets were written in succession and immediately staged in Leningrad: "The Golden Age" (1930), "Bolt" (1931) and "Bright Rivulet" (1935). The destiny of all three was unfortunate and all for the one reason: the scenarios were ineptly done, primitive in content and unattractive.

Though the history of each ballet has separate nuances, "Bright Rivulet" was best staged (ballet-master Fyodor Lopukhov) and the choreography contained quite a few interesting moments. The script makes the ballet into typical country vaudeville that is highly flippant and comprises age-old comic situations. A ballet company comes to a collective farm in the countryside to perform. The farmers' team-leader gets involved with one of the dancers, not knowing that his own wife had trained at ballet school in her youth along with the object of his attentions. And some of the other country folk are charmed by the ballerinas. Naturally, everything ends up for the good. The script was politely condemned by all the critics who noted confusion in the sequence of the plot, old-fashioned characters who are larger than life, and the lack of taste in some of the comic episodes.

But for all its faults, "Bright Rivulet" was originally planned as vaudeville which is a genre with its own special standards. Things went worse with the ballet "Bolt" where the script was meant to address a serious theme but despite that disintegrated into vaudeville and a parody of the grave content. The main character was loafer and drunkard Lyonka Gulba who was sacked from the factory where he worked. In revenge he talked a youth into putting a bolt into a tool and this would blow up the works. The conspiracy obviously does not come off and justice wins out.

That's a summary of the scenario but the action is dragged out over three acts and extremely wanly or, to quote one critic of that time, "pretty well senselessly." The intrigue and conflict only come out in the third act and in another five minutes are brought to a favorable conclusion. The first two acts constituted protracted genre productions repeating time-old means of entertainment. The script got bogged down in demonstrative social contrasts where good and bad characters collide head-on. Some characters are cast all in white and the rest all in black, which is somewhat surreal.

But "The Golden Age" is our main theme. Its script too did not exactly glow. Capitalism has named a major industrial exhibition "The Golden Age" and there it demonstrates its achievements, of which a murderous gun of huge proportions is considered the greatest. A Soviet soccer team attends the entertainment side of the exhibition. The host country is camouflaged and not identified by any specific national features but it is ruled entirely by Fascists. They are frightened to see the football in the hands of the leader of the Soviet team, taking it for a bomb and the "hand of Moscow." The music-hall dancer is also a Fascist and tries to compromise the leader of the Soviet group but to no avail. Then the Fascists plant papers in his hotel room and arrest him and his colleagues. The Soviet athletes dash to the prison, freeing him and all the other inmates. The performance is then rounded off with a dance of solidarity.

This first script for "The Golden Age" is typical of its times in its global aspirations and naive ideas. Thus was expressed an ardent and misguided belief that worldwide revolution was nigh. This superficial sociological symbolism tended toward primitivism. All the action on alien soil was clothed in window-dressing. The performances of the Soviet athletes, their fight for justice and their fast-achieved union with the proletariat of another land all led to ostentation. Events were confused and bit by bit lost logic.

Both "Bolt" (choreography F. Lopukhov) and "The Golden Age" (choreography V. Vainonen, L. Jacobson and V. Chesnokov) included individual choreographic innovations but the overall impression was poor due to the primitive scenarios. For all the efforts, the ballets were just not dramatic. The most curious thing is that "The Golden Age" scenario was discussed in the press before it was staged and deemed unacceptable for ballet, and the critics said the same about "Bolt." Moreover, the dance version of "The Golden Age" was delayed by Shostakovich and stage director Alexander Gauk as needing more work on the script. But, as we see today, there was no point in refining a script that was simply unsuitable for ballet.

Today we can but wonder why it was necessary to accept weak scripts unsuitable for ballet dancing. Yet such was the need of a moment when the art was in a trough.

The Russia that had just accomplished the world's first socialist revolution was thirsting for new forms in all spheres of life, and that included literature and the arts. New ideas were born in prose, drama, poetry, the cinema and painting. The contemporary world needed a modern language, and ballet began to seem an anachronism with its passion for myths, fairy-tales, and sylphides, elves, princes and princesses. Already the voices of overzealous supporters of proletarian culture (wrongly identified as something apart from all tradition) were calling for ballet to be dropped from the ship of modern life as an art belonging to courtiers and the aristocracy, as something distanced from real life, incomprehensible for a revolutionary people and not needed by them (though ordinary folk had displayed an inclination for ballet). So ballet theaters set out to prove their right to exist, tried to take on new social themes related to modern times.

The most intriguing thing is that the script for "The Golden Age" was selected in a competition announced by the Leningrad Opera Theater (once known as the Marinsky Theater and now as the Kirov). One shudders to think of the standard of the other librettos if the one chosen was so poor. There was no experience. For experience, ballet turned to drama where, at that time, shows were being put on to arouse the revolutionary ideas in people: there were inevitably such characters as the capitalist, worker, villain, saboteur, etc. Some brilliant images were born but drama is after all the product of Literature and as such has a different system of methods and instruments. The refined and symbolic art of ballet could not just directly adopt such methods and forget its own musical form which requires real life to be expressed in poetry. Hence ballet became a mere semblance of itself, gross, and common, two-instead of three-dimensional.

Shostakovich, in accepting the script outline proposed, improved it (as had happend before with Tchaikovsky) a hundred times over by letting his music take a totally different scale. The virtues of his music were noted in the reviews of all the ballets, just as was the gap between music and plot. The choreographers were captive to the libretto.

All three ballet shows soon closed.

With time the shadow of failure affected the music too. The newspaper critics had given it just a few words and with the passing of time it became difficult to judge since Shostakovich's ballet pieces were not published. They did exist on gramophone records and infrequently a small medley of themes from his ballets was performed. The theme taken from "The Golden Age" consisted, for example, of just four pieces.

Bias was strong and fear of risk was greater than it should have been in writing about the happenings of those times. At any rate this impeded the choreographers from the outset. No one dreamed of returning Shostakovich's ballets to the stage. Later came other obstacles. The originals of the ballets of the great composer in effect ceased to exist as integral works. The pages settled into archives topsy-turvy. Were they all there? Was nothing lost? An answer to such questions required lengthy search with unpredictable results. Enthusiasts were needed.

Quest for "The Golden Age"

Moscow has, apart from the Bolshoi, one more opera and ballet company. It has been named "The Stanislavsky and Nemirovich-Danchenko Musical Theater." The two famous stage directors honored in its name (Stanislavsky also founded a system of training actors that won world recognition) gave part of their time to developing musical theater. And the theater mentioned above was originally born of a fusion of the opera companies they had established. In 1933 a ballet group joined and the Theater took on its contemporary form. Unlike the Bolshoi, which specializes in big operas and ballets, the junior partner looks for chamber pieces and gives precedence to works by modern authors that are more about life today.

But such an intent is not so easy to achieve, for composers do not so often make operas and ballets on a contemporary theme. The Stanislavsky and Nemirovich-Danchenko Musical Theater likes to present works about real life though on occasion it performs abstract, symbolic ballets with no special theme. That diversion does not erode the main repertoire emphasis. The Theater's plans for the future generally include "ballet on contemporary subjects," the clear purpose being new themes.

One example is provided by the year 1974 when Director Mikhail Yurovsky and Sergei Sapozhnikov, a music historian and spare-time composer working as a consultant, came up with the idea of resurrecting the forgotten ballet music of Shostakovich's "The Golden Age" and "Bolt." They approached the composer who reacted to the revival plans somewhat sceptically. He hadn't the notes or scores of his ballets and had no idea as to their archive condition. But his scepticism came rather from the doubt as to whether ballets he had written so long ago could have a new stage life. Still, Shostakovich did not reject the enthusiasts, giving them access to his personal archives where some originals might be located.

For the most part the materials ought to have been in the Leningrad archives, and especially in the library of the Kirov Theater where the ballets had been performed. Sapozhnikov and Yurovsky as knowledgeable music people realized what they had let themselves in for but even they were shocked by the degree of difficulty involved. The materials were in such a chaotic condition that it was hard to say even how much time would be spent on sorting them out. The new stage version had to be ready by a definite date. Their plans had to be altered.

But Sapozhnikov was so taken by the business at hand that he resolved to pursue it whatever time was involved and to restore at least the music of the first Shostakovich ballet, "The Golden Age." He chose not to look too far ahead to whether or not it would actually be staged and set himself the goal of filling in a gap in the legacy of the great composer. At that time Sapozhnikov worked with Muzika publishers and devoted his spare time to finding the lost ballet. This led to a whole expedition that lasted about five years. Music enthusiasts from the archive section also got involved, along with young composers and note transcribers. Most active of all were the staff of the Kirov Theater's library. Gradually the scattered fragments of the score, clavier numbers and individual orchestra pieces from "The Golden Age" were gathered together, given system and welded into one whole. This was far from easy to do. Some pages of "The Golden Age" had vanished into files containing other works. And the files with "The Golden Age" contained scores from other works. Some pieces were found without name or index. In such cases the researcher had to determine whether they belonged to the ballet at hand and in what place. Sometimes there were two or three headings for one and the same episode and it was necessary to ascertain which was right. And not always did the sequence coincide with the notes and stage play.

Sapozhnikov has original schedules crossed out as each part of the work was accomplished. All the orchestral pieces were assembled. All the scores were found; all the clavier numbers. And every section in the schedule has empty squares; some numbers exist only in the clavier version, others only as scores and a third set merely as orchestral voices. The Theater library's stock turned out to be incomplete. Part of the gap was filled from the Shostakovich home library. Some scores were nowhere to be found at all and were restored on the basis of the orchestral parts. Nine clavier numbers were also not found and the young composers redid them.

At length all was ready. It had taken gargantuan work, unselfish volunteer labor. Sapozhnikov inspired and led that effort. He said: "By way of comparison, we might say that, in hunting down and raising from the ruins parts buried under dust and disintegrated through time, we're restoring a building. The major outcome was that the ballet music was there and had not been lost beyond trace. But that was just the first stage of the work. Now the assembled fabric needed to be decorated; the versions needed checking along with the music "text" and the mistakes that inevitably make their way into manuscripts had to be weeded out . . . And that's exactly what we were about. As everyone knows, there were no printed notes . . . "

What Sapozhnikov mentions demands the most scrupulous, painstaking work, filigree precision and a fine sense of music. That side of things was undertaken by a pupil of Shostakovich, the famous composer Benjamin Basner. The current score includes amendments made by Shostakovich after the 1930 première. There is evidence to prove this. Some pages are dated and a large number of the amendments are to the orchestral tones and sounds, which means they could only have come after an orchestra was heard by a large audience during a performance of the ballet.

Most unfortunately, Shostakovich himself did not live to see the fruit of all this work. He passed away in 1975 and the hard graft to rebuild "The Golden Age" was completed only in 1980.

The Return of the "Golden Age"

And so the original score became a dossier of music paper. Then the wife of Dmitry Shostakovich, Irina, herself at one time an editor with a music publisher, asked Yuri Grigorovich to return "The Golden Age" to the stage. Her choice of Grigorovich was natural for here was a man of true talent, the top Soviet choreographer whose every production brought something new to the ballet world. When the Bolshoi Theater toured Britain in the summer of 1986, well-known critic Mary Clark wrote that Grigorovich the choreographer could only be outdone by Grigorovich the person. And that's true. Grigorovich's innovative powers have attracted people in the most diverse countries.

The great Shostakovich had a high opinion of the choreographer and was quick to spot his talent. When at 30 years of age Grigorovich produced his first major work, "The Stone Flower," Shostakovich praised it in the press, thereafter following the career of the young ballet-master and reviewing other of his works. Composer and choreographer became friends and would meet to chat. Grigorovich always dreamed of staging a Shostakovich ballet and secretly hoped the composer would write a new work. But he could not bring himself to speak of this to Shostakovich, remembering the pain ballet had unjustly brought to him. And Shostakovich was occupied with most serious symphonic works. Yet fate was to bring the ballet-master his greatest dream.

Grigorovich was absolutely delighted with the idea of staging "The Golden Age" and took it up with great vigor. He arranged for the Bolshoi Theater to study the original scores of the ballet and in the spring of 1981 the music from "The Golden Age" was first performed orchestrally. It was a working performance before a few musicians and composers. For all that, it was a big event. After half a century of silence, justice triumphed and "The Golden Age" was resurrected, at least as a work of music. It was the first step in a new lease on life for it, a first gala after oblivion. But the work to return the ballet to the stage had only just begun.

Intense efforts got underway. The old scenario was rejected completely and a new one written by Grigorovich accompanied by a friend of Shostakovich's, the music historian Isaac Glikman, who had seen the first performance of "The Golden Age" way back in 1930.

The new script had Love as one of the central themes. The script writers proceeded from ballet being principally an art telling of people's feelings. And isn't love the supreme human sentiment, the one that makes the world go round? That had always been Shostakovich's view on ballet. And lyrics, penetrating at that, had occupied no minor place in his work. The old "The Golden Age" script had been politically tendentious in the extreme and had had no place for lyrics. That clearly fettered the composer. True, he had found a way round those narrow bounds and lyrical moments made their way into the music anyway. But there were not enough of them and the decision was taken to supplement the score with fragments from other Shostakovich compositions close in style and spirit to "The Golden Age" and written around the same time. The ballet now includes a piece from the music for "The Human Comedy," and the Adagio from the First and Second Concertos for Fortepiano: to this music the lyrical duets of the main characters, Rita and Boris, are set.

Shostakovich himself had made such a transfer of theme material from one work to another. For example, "The Golden Age" has the theme from the finale of his First Concerto for Fortepiano. Prokofiev and Tchaikovsky had done the like too. The insertions in "The Golden Age" have been made with the utmost of taste and tact. Composers such as Georgy Sviridov are enraptured.

All that work and the actual staging of the ballet took something over a year. The set was made by artist Simon Virsaladze, a constant partner of Grigorovich. Yuri Simonov (then the Chief Conductor with the Bolshoi Theater) and young assistant Alexander Lavrenok (himself a soloist in past years with the Bolshoi) saw to the orchestra.

The première of "The Golden Age" came November 4, 1982. It was an outstanding success that evoked rave reviews.

Grigorovich's "The Golden Age"

Yuri Grigorovich had some experience in reviving ballets before he took on "The Golden Age." He had made a success of Sergei Prokofiev's "The Stone Flower" where other ballet-masters had failed.

The Prokofiev ballet first hit the stage in 1954 at the Bolshoi. The choreography was by Leonid Lavrovsky, one of the top men in the field. Past merits did not help as the production slumped down and out in less than a season. This happens infrequently in the Soviet Union where any production that enjoys some degree of public interest is usually guaranteed quite a long run. Three years later, in 1957, Yuri Grigorovich at age 30 showed the illustrious Lavrovsky how "The Stone Flower" should be produced. The victory of the ballet was the greater for its being the young choreographer's first big ballet as a professional. It was a roaring success that made him a star overnight. Time has confirmed that status. Even today, Grigorovich's version of "The Stone Flower" is being staged in Moscow and Leningrad, and enjoys its former popularity. The choreographer has presented it all over the country and abroad in Stockholm, Sweden.

He did something similar with Aram Khachaturian's "Spartacus." Leonid Jacobson, a ballet-master of the old generation, made only a minor success of it in Leningrad in 1957. Individual scenes and dances attracted but the overall impression was spoiled by the main characters, Spartacus and Crassus, not dancing but posing solely in mime. The performance lost its flow and integrality. Grigorovich again fixed things. His revised version in Moscow 1968 can be said without exaggeration to be an immense hit. It runs to this day, never failing to captivate audiences with the majestic power and virtuoso beauty of the male dances.

And history kept repeating itself: where others failed, Grigorovich scored stunning successes. Great talent is the explanation or perhaps more precisely a special feature of Grigorovich's gift. For he is the most musical of all Soviet ballet-masters. He has the ability to hear in the music something nobody has ever sensed before. This is what gives his productions fresh and innovative ideas, concepts and images. A ballet that failed previously gains a new choreographic and dramatic interpretation under him which opens up the depth of the content. True, up to "The Golden Age," Grigorovich was able to keep some of the original choreography and some part of the original script. In "Spartacus" or "The Stone Flower," for example, he was correcting the stage version to make it correspond to what he heard in the music.

The work he undertook with "The Golden Age" was much more complex. He could not just amend and alter it. The old script was utterly unacceptable, needing total recasting to make it fit the music. A daunting task.

There were plenty of skeptics to say the job was impossible and not worth tackling. They asserted that if the music had been written for a specific literary setting, nothing else could be played to that music. Grigorovich, like any bright talent, has his foes and rivals as well as well-wishers. They publicly showed doubts and, whether they realized it or not, their motivation was purely egotistic. For them it would be better if Grigorovich sat idle, for each work by him always held the risk of success.

The arrows were being fired at the choreographer and were hitting the composer too. Such an attitude was forever denying access to the theater for the Shostakovich ballets which were fast receding into oblivion: only up on the stage can music composed for ballet achieve its full potential and richness.

Grigorovich did not enter into vain discussion, convinced that only the end performance could answer the doubts. He was seeking the right choreography for the Shostakovich music in his ear. The more he listened to that music, the gladder he was, for it sounded fresh and contemporary. The devices used had been ahead of their day and fitted the modern music panorama. At the same time, the music had captured perfectly the tone of the Twenties when the Soviet Union was being formed. Shostakovich catches the voice of the street, big square, the bustling crowd, the expanse from the closed world of solitary life. Such had been the times when "The Golden Age" was born. Philosophical reflections on the history in the making then and psychological awareness came later. At that initial moment when Russia had taken the sharp turn into a new way of life, strong feelings prevailed, great passions and an exceptionally poignant choice. The fight between old and new, regardless of the sphere of human life where it takes place, always requires clarity, precise positions, exact shades of color. Therein lies the pathos of the struggle and the optimism which reigned supreme in the early days. At the base of the struggle, a great battle between good and evil is omnipresent; and there is always an ardent, passionate belief that good will defeat evil and life will win over death.

Such was the outlook of those long-gone, bright and turbulent Twenties in the land of Soviets. This was the world view expressed, for instance, by the film reels of Sergei Eisenstein or the plays of Vsevolod Meierhold. That inspiration is personified in the music of "The Golden Age" as composed by the 24-year-old Shostakovich, despite the first script of 1930. That script, at first glance, seemed to show general patterns, notably the struggle between the old and new world in the international arena, but was enmeshed by a sociologically primitive plot. Hence the breadth of intents was given a demonstrative and narrow form and engendered boredom.

Shostakovich went from breadth to depth like the true artist he was even then. The most paradoxical thing is that he seemed to submit to the scenario, leaving in the score the names of episodes lacking in guile such as:

Negro-Fascist Boxing Match;
Dance of the Tennis-Players;
Soviet Team Workout; etc.

Yet for the composer these were merely external contours into which he would breathe life. And listening to the music you get to thinking that this veritable revelation could hardly be about boxers or footballers. The music is miles above such themes. Instead of representing ostentatious displays in some flamboyant country of the West, Shostakovich has produced an amazing and grand sound image of his own nation at the turning-point of the Twenties.

He transforms into art the things that distinguished that era—the gay melodies of the ditties, the drumming beat of the march, the crisp style of the physical training session, the perky, rousing intonations of the newborn Soviet songs. Thus Shostakovich catches the rhythm of the Twenties, the world outlook then, the emotional pathos of a country rebuilding from scratch. In other words he draws a definite picture. Such is one level in music where openness, directness and enthusiasm predominate. The ardor of youth coming of age and affirming its place in the world. The music tells of life brimming with passionate outbursts of romanticism, with bright hopes, fervor and with racing and unexpected presentiments of alarm and dramatic tension.

Another musical world is represented by the tango rhythms, foxtrots and shimmies that came to Russia from the West and were very popular in the theater and folk festivities. The old script, as we've mentioned, was blatant in portraying in plain black the corruption of a bourgeois society overrun with Fascists and busy 'round the clock preparing sabotage against the Soviet athletes. The idea "bourgeois" did not boil down to the political notion dictated by the script. Shostakovich was intrigued by bourgeois life as a vulgar, narrow outlook, as meaning spiritual emasculation. This theme occupied him all his days and was developed all the long years he composed. "The Golden Age" contains dances popular at that time which he wittily and craftily parodies. There are roaming, affectedly approximate intonations and murderously mechanical rhythms and then, quite the opposite, wan, fatigued breaks in the melody with shrill rises and descending, seemingly false sounds . . . Thus forms the general picture of life as uncultured and fatigued but camouflaged in window-dressing. That impotence holds hidden danger. Suddenly threatening notes appear, a music latently gloomy that bears bad tidings—still the one theme cutting through two others.

The different layers of music are for different phenomena in life. Comparison shows their essential incompatibility—moral, spiritual and psychological. Shostakovich expresses in this work a deep content, profound thoughts, and the tension of fates crumbling and forming. A far cry from cut-and-dried sociological presentations or one-dimensional posters. And the music knows no drabness. It has much bright wit, sparkling irony, humor, and fastidiously fine flight of fantasy.

This is the music of a young composer with mature and sensitive thought and fine intuition (we might note that in his youth Shostakovich wrote the tragic opera "Katerina Izmailova"). He is a person genuinely open to life, eagerly taking in all its voices and colors. And the music speaks of a young country starting out. Life promised a fine tomorrow and people were lulled into thinking that the festivities would never end. The heat of struggle washed with that naive belief brought people a penetrating joy and their soul delighted in their involvement in the great changes coming about. This very atmosphere and spirit lives in the music of "The Golden Age" which reflects that era in history.

The young Shostakovich at the time of the creation of the ballet.

Grigorovich created the choreographic version on the basis of that deep sense in Shostakovich's work. But first, of course, a stage script was devised. As we mentioned, the script was redone but in such a way as to maintain a link with the former one.

As script writers, Grigorovich and Glikman acted just as the composer had in his time. In thinking up the new plot, they remained within the limits of the old libretto, the conditions set for the music.

Naturally the times remain the same, the place being changed from foreign to domestic. This the music needed. This meant people would be seen in full three dimensions, instead of in outlines. The script-writers can be said to have transferred the characters, live beings, of the former libretto back from their trip abroad to their native home. Without dropping sport, they have come to art, being amateur actors. As fishermen they now have a profession. There is one and the same group of young people but their destiny has gained extra features.

It was more difficult to find something to contrast the first. Grigorovich finds an excellent way out. The figure 1923 is written on the decor. The Russian viewer thereby understands that these are the times of the New Economic Policy as indicated in the new libretto. That Policy was introduced by Lenin to allow private enterprise in some areas of the national economy. This was a special, complex and most interesting period in the history of the Land of Soviets when there were different class groups alongside each other. The proprietary class lingered on into the era of proletarian power.

The current script has gathered the "bygones" under the one roof of a nightclub called "The Golden Age" where the old lifestyle is having a final fling.

But a dramatic situation was needed to get the story going. And something boisterous and venturesome, as dynamic as the whirlwind music with its sudden contrasts and kaleidoscopic events. So, in the new script, "The Golden Age" variety club is a bandit den. The owner, dancer Monsieur Jacques, is the ringleader, and is known there as Yashka. The fishermen by coincidence come into contact with these people and, sensing something suspicious, chase them, lose the trail and then find it again. In the end the band is broken up.

The situation is also fired by a love story. The star of the club, Jacques's dancing partner Rita, falls in love with the young fisherman Boris. She is totally unaware of what goes on behind the scenes at "The Golden Age" and ends up involuntarily the center of controversy as Jacques demands her love. And Lyuska, Jacques's gangster contact, has a crush on him. This is how the plot is cleverly woven.

The script is deftly tailored for ballet. There is a minimum of secondary events which means the action is easy to grasp. And there is plenty of scope for the choreography. That language, deep and rich in associations, complements the plot.

Chapter 2

Dawn of a New Lifestyle

An orchestral overture rings out gay and fanciful to herald events out of the ordinary. The curtain is only just beginning to rise but action is already in full swing on stage. We seem to catch it at its height with the sun pouring down onto a square, flags flying wildly and a colorful crowd engaged in animated, bright movement. The libretto says briefly: popular festivities. But Grigorovich expands on this expression. On stage is life itself bubbling and flowing. That life is multi-dimensional. Colors change magically like in a kaleidoscope and we get what are fragments from different human biographies.

A bold seaman performs a tap dance. A girl selling cigarettes is flirting with him. A waif meanwhile mimics them, acting the fool. A newspaper boy canters about as though a cavalier. These characters keep asserting themselves in short dances, coming out of the crowd only to fuse with it again and again. The general flow of life surrounds them.

At each new twist in the overall action more characters appear. Out onto the square come athletes to perform. Grigorovich presents their sporting performance in an open-ended dance composition with easily recognizable sports motion. We see the runners overtaking each other, the swimmers swallow-diving, and the acrobats forming pyramids. There are discus-throwers, rowers and even gliders.

A further splash of the crowd and a new aspect of life unfolds before us. The athletes are replaced by a youth theater company. They gaily play out the following: young folk astride brooms chase a general, clergyman and business person.

And so the first scene of the ballet forms out of a number of reprises, episodes and groups of movement differing in dance language and genre. But all this spicy diversity possesses the same feverish excitement and mirth and is joined by the one dynamic rhythm. All the world seems to be present at the day of genesis and furiously trying out its strength. This is Life with tantalizing opportunities. Youth in the doorway of destiny. Through the festivities Grigorovich's choreography and drama produce multiple associations.

Each of the three acts of "The Golden Age" has one such mass scene (with youth only). They are continuations which paint a general image and the common destiny of the new generation that is starting out.

If at the beginning of the performance we saw young strength and talents being merrily tried out, in the second act the life that bubbled so riotously is looked at from within, and work and love become the most important things. Grigorovich has worked an original choreographic novella where the story line is that the fishermen have gone to sea and their girlfriends await them on the shore.

The dances of the fishermen have clever working elements sown in and we can see them drawing their nets and setting the sails . . . The dances of the fishermen reproduce a seascape. The danseuses are carried high to produce the image of seagulls and sailing ships. The corps de ballet do the running waves. And all the male dancing is filled with fresh gusts of wind. A picturesque and gallant beauty proceed from the bold virtuosity, impetuosity and springiness of the male parts.

Grigorovich expresses the poetic ideal of labor fused with nature. The dance shows the bold human spirit which fears not the elements. There is relentless energy drawing the romantics on to the unknown. Then one realizes the deft skill that prompted the choice of the fishing profession for the ballet. The sea produces a bright theatrical metaphor, is a symbol of youth, vitality, daring and romanticism . . .

And on the shore are the girls waiting and doing their round dances. These are light and flitting with the exquisite twitter of pas-de-point, a soft, transparent picture where the classical pattern has elements of Russian dance folklore neatly entwined.

The life of these young men and women is natural and harmoniously blends with their native land and age-old traditions, with simple but geniune and strong sentiments. And that lifestyle, showing its inner essence, has captivating purity and deep human aspirations for love, happiness and constructive deeds.

The third and final mass youth scene concludes the performance. Once again there is a gala in the square. Unlike the first one at the start of the ballet, here there are no people of different outlook and all are dancing in the same style. There has been a fusion of the classical and sporting movements. But this united corps de ballet performs in groups, each with a different number of dancers and each with its picture in dance. Some race around in a circle, others cut through diagonally, and a third group is jumping. Everything is in motion at the one time. That motion speeds, gains impetus and expands. The variety of impulses are blended by a joyful sentiment of oneness of purpose. All is pointed high and far. Here is the conquering energy, spirit and courage. It's like a flight into future time. One feels the winged dream of youth which knows no alarm or doubts and is enchanted by the brilliance of life and its boundless horizons.

All three mass scenes contain the hero of the ballet—Boris. He is the deftest of the athletes and the most striking player in the amateur theater. He flies like a free bird o'er the waves in the sea scene and is the most purposeful in the final parade. His role is filled throughout with virtuoso dancing involving high leaps and bold flights with stunning turns in the air. All this happens at breakneck speed though strict, precise, sculpted lines and postures are expressed. The sporting and acrobatic methods are set off by the form of classical dance. The virtuosity and dynamics of the dance of the main character grow from scene to scene. And if Spartacus in its time was the highest standard in male dance, the role of Boris must claim that position today. His dancing is the culmination of the mass scenes and the choreography also becomes more and more complex and full of flight with each new act. Boris is the leader of the new generation, the embodiment of an ideal born of life. And he is the ideal hero of the entire performance, the moral and spiritual center. A fine and fearless knight personifying spirit, inspiration and aspiration. He is a fighter and romantic.

Grigorovich's choreography is mutli-tiered. There is the symbolic content of youth as a whole regardless of birth and social position; of youth at all times thirsting for new knowledge. And the ballet is by no means abstract. A definite era and country come through with great vitality: the Twenties and the young Land of Soviets . . .   The choreographer has combined the theme of young people and young country. Any viewer anywhere can, from the moment the curtain goes up, guess that the nation is just beginning to build. The definiteness bears a clearly theatrical character since the features of the time and country are conveyed through images from art in those years, images familiar in terms of art, cinema, theater and literature . . .

The theatrical constructivism of the Twenties is captured in the fine decor of Simon Virsaladze: surfaces of varying sizes and light mobile frames canvased over. They are so real as at times to seem part of the pattern of the dance. Uneven letters and numbers staring out like fragments of posters. This is the decor principle for the whole performance.

The time and place of the action can also be guessed by the costumes. Young men in overalls; girls in sporty dresses with red headscarves as was the fashion of Young Communist women at the time. And the seaman, waif, cigarette girl and paperboy are all real images of the people of those first years of Soviet government. They seem to have come straight out of the paintings and cinema reels and into the ballet in groups set in among the general dance: the newspaper boy and the inquisitive Young Communist girls crowding round him in their red headscarves; the smiling sailor and the waif looking awefully at him; Young Communists and in the center young men in army hats . . . The athletes reproduce in the ballet the theatricalized physical training movements popular at the dawn of Soviet government. We also see reincarnated (in the first part of "The Golden Age") the large-scale street parties and festivities.

The characteristic political theater of the time is restored by the choreographer. Such theaters usually enjoyed the abbreviated name of TRAM (Working Youth Theater). They possessed open revolutionary pathos and played using extremely demonstrative devices. In his young years Shostakovich worked with such a group in Leningrad and wrote the music for three of its pieces. He also collaborated with Vsevolod Meierhold, the famous director whose esthetic program was adopted by the TRAMs. Incidentally, the scene portrayed by the TRAM players in Grigorovich's ballet reflects in minor detail the echos of the Civil War which had just been concluded and marked another turning-point in the life of the nation.

Thus throughout the ballet Grigorovich keeps the symbolic sense in tune with real life.

Intriguing Metamorphoses

"The Golden Age" as a ballet presents a serious theme in an acute, bright and grasping frame. This is a work where not only the plot is a detective tale with the usual chases, fights and revelation of the villains. Grigorovich has managed to make the story truly theatrical and suited to ballet. The whole system of modes of expression is brought into adventurous play.

The characters are dual as in the best thrillers. And long before the action really takes off, the main personages are clearly out of a detective tale. No sooner have we seen a modest Rita in the square than she suddenly appears in the variety show as the flamboyant prima donna. The elegant dancer Monsieur Jacques, her partner, turns out to be the gang ringleader Yashka. And the languid, worldly woman of the restaurant is his girl Lyuska.

True, unlike in drama, the viewer receives a program before the start of the ballet telling the secrets of the plot and which of the main characters is hiding behind which mask. But then we go to drama theaters to see the works, say, of Shakespeare which we have known since school age. In art what is important is not so much what happens but how it came to be and how that is shown. And hence my emphasis that Grigorovich has created a profoundly theatrical and ballet-suited thriller where our attention is on how the events came to pass. And, forgive my repeating myself, the script is excellently conceived so that the main action really stands out.

We are informed of the events of the plot but, without seeing the movement, we could not imagine when these things happened: the choreography expands them and gives them dimension, framing them in the vast mass scenes. All the details, nuances and accents are sealed in the choreography which itself produces adventure which makes the performance captivating throughout. With each turn we get new modes of dance. The dance seems to sharpen, cutting deceptive illusions, intriguing us with the transformations and multiplicity in one and the same phenomenon and the unexpected oneness of different phenomena.

The dancing is subtly edged, has bravura and virtuosity. Dizzy acrobatic cascades are welded alongside classical movement. And the dancing is sylph-like, airy and transparent. These different styles both belong to one role in "The Golden Age," Rita. This meeting of styles is what choreography is all about: choosing and soul-searching make the image.

The dance of Rita's part tears out of elegance into free-style. The abrasiveness of her dance in the club scenes acquires smoothness in the scenes in the square and by the sea. The effective flights and holds pass into haughty, garish poses. There are exquisite change-abouts to grandiose, ingenuous motions . . . Rita, breaking out of "The Golden Age" and into freedom, enjoys the liberty. But, experiencing this peak, she is drawn back again to the romantic fantasies of theater.

Rita, the star of the showclub, is invisibly separated from her public by dancing in which regal boldness does not break the harmony. She is an enigmatic figure, a hostage of art not affected by mundaneness.

For her "The Golden Age" is the world of theater and not crass show business. Here on the stage she performs sparkling and dangerous turns. There, by the wide blue sea and her beloved one, she finds peace and reconciliation. This role of a modern heroine is reminiscent of the romantic Odetta in "The Swan Lake." But this is the first time that a dual romantic image has been woven around a contemporary plot and based on modern choreographic material. And Grigorovich in "The Golden Age" presents not one but a whole series of such roles on a principle each time uniquely and originally his for just about all the leading characters. This, I would say, is what gives the choreography its detective tint where it constantly changes.

This is a new departure for classical ballet, an extra aspect. It has a poignancy and acerbity all its own. But here, in comparison with the dances of Rita, all has grown shallow and broken, lost its nobility of line.

Refinement is reborn as gaudiness, and style as garishness. Classical ballet seems to be parodying itself. The incarnation of this is Lyuska, a personage for whom the classical language is distorted and broken. Here the dancing intrigues, balancing on the brink of passing over to another profession. And this in the final analysis happens: before us is another type of dance which has monstrously assumed everyday gestures and even karate methods. Here Lyuska is in character, without the carnival mask adorned for the restaurant. Now there is no shadow of her former wan and tender languidness. All is full of biting sharpness, crude force and predatory energy.

Lyuska's role is quite unconventional. A big part for a ballerina yet the form is mocking and grotesque. In whimsical combinations of dance methods the character is opened up.

Grigorovich's choreography is crafty. It makes captivating mirages and then reveals them caustically. The elegant splendor of the tango so characteristic of Monsieur Jacques bewitches and charms. But as soon as the number is over, the lights at "The Golden Age" go out and in the wings another life-form begins. The white gloves, bow-tie, morning-coat and top-hat come off agonizingly slowly . . . Each gesture is protracted in the extreme and emphatically significant. An ominous ritual is being run through. The measured rhythm is hypnotic and holds all in bated expectation. Monsieur Jacques is not simply removing his stage clothes; he is changing face. The stage personality has done his bit and now we get wild hopping instead of a filigree tango. This is the baring of a soul tired of playing to cabaret. Here the dance barbarically parodies the lounge style of the nightclub, satirizes wickedly, with a vengeance.

Even such an integral character as Boris is given a chance to experience a dual condition as he plays a caricature tsarist general in the square.

The choreography attracts with its unexpected turns, play of diverse forms, and the bold contrasts of grotesque and lyrics, satire and pathetic elements, drama and comedy. And deep down the dance episodes also frequently contain a duality. Take, for example, Rita's tango with her partner in Act Three. For the regulars at "The Golden Age," this is the latest exotic act of their idol. But for her this is breaking-point, a moment full of drama and life when she decides finally to quit the cabaret scenes. A farewell tango, where behind the usual constrained stage smile the soul is buzzing.

Or take the very next episode. Rita, rejecting Yashka's love, witnessing Lyuska's death and finally realizing what is concealed behind the scenes at "The Golden Age," is taken hostage by the gang. And here on the stage appears the revue apachee, a marvelous innovation by the choreographer. The club regulars take it as a spellbinding new number. In fact the stage performance hides a real situation. Yashka and his men, before an unsuspecting public, are with impunity threatening Rita. The gang close in on and surround their latest victim, shut off the way to safety. But the ringleader with an irresistible smile encourages the public as it wildly applauds Rita, little suspecting that she is indeed in the clutches of brigands and is really calling for help.

And the full variety of character metamorphoses are more than just gripping in themselves. The choreographer uses them to intensify the intrigue. He includes Rita, for instance, in the chase scene in Act Two. Hence the chased at the one time become chasers. The heroine is caught in a dangerous web which she knows nothing about. The gang have recognized her. Yashka has time to hide his face in a mask and the rest are unknown to her just as the events behind the facade of "The Golden Age." The action thus gains a dual tension.

The duality of what is presented in the ballet is beautifully shown in artist Virsaladze's scenography. The mobile and easily interchangeable back-props and canvas sails, cones and canvas pennants enable the action to transfer with lightning speed from one world to another, from the square to the nightclub, and from there to the seashore . . . All life is apparently changeable.

The costumes tell the same story: the jackets of the men are multi-colored just as are their trousers, and the women have stockings of opposite colors and there is a contrast of two colors in their dress . . . The artist also gives the action a virtually surreal tinge, taking it to the very border of reality and imagination.

The ballet sparks and plays. There is never a minute without surprises that are effective and spectacular. Each and every moment has a detective nature from plot, drama, dance, and art. The sharp social issue is presented engagingly (just as Shostakovich, incidentally, always insisted it should be) and loses none of its depth or seriousness for this. The well-conceived theatricalized elements reveal the full dramatism of the destinies of the main characters. The features, problems and conflicts of those times are clearly shown, times when the wind of revolutionary change stirred all former life. Some were swept aside and others raised. That wind confused and mixed up former notions, presented a choice, and forced people to seek their place in a world being reborn. Unimaginably long roads were spun.

In "The Golden Age" that whole whirlpool of human quests and complexities of life revolves. We have the romantics of the revolution such as Boris, and the time-servers like Yashka. There are people such as Rita seeking and finding their way in the new lifestyle and others like Lyuska losing their way, floundering and grasping at straws. The image of the era is theatrically expanded in the personal destinies of the characters.

"The Golden Age" has brought to Soviet ballet theater a new approach to material about contemporary life. The modern theme has acquired an engrossing new genre and a serious, dramatically acute content that is bright and spectacular. The variety of dance forms and types is unconventional for contemporary ballet.

The exemplary choreography, richness of the dance, and neatly intensifying composition is reminiscent of the great classic "The Sleeping Beauty" with music by Pyotr Tchaikovsky and choreography by Marius Petipa.

The Secrets of Night

Life comes across in this ballet in the formation, play, and battle of many colors and different forces. We might say the light of bright new days is shining forth to pierce the temptations and menace of night. And the opposite force comes on just like a symphony, moving against the theme of light.

The festive square had only just been alight, the flags playing in the sun and boundless space beckoning. And now mousy-gray conical frames cut down the space, the light grows dull and wan, and out come the words "The Golden Age" in gilded letters. In the shade of flickering lamps a shadowy world is going by, attracting with a languid beauty, the slow rhythms of the tango and a tempting parade of "the girls" led by a feverishly prancing Master of Ceremonies . . . This is the image of the old lifestyle, a passing world. And these mass scenes in the cabaret alternate all through the ballet with the mass youth scenes, comparing and contrasting.

Hence everything is straining to fly off, bouncing with energy. In these restaurant episodes we see pretentiousness, airs and graces, and breakdown. Here life is agonizing in the sparks of a desperate last fling complete with the rousing cancan and the mournful, melancholy, elegaic tango.

There is the world of natural sentiments. And the dance is full of sporting, folklore, and everyday rhythm. Here the world is doomed, artificial, condemned.

This is brilliantly conveyed in the scene that opens Act Two. We see a dance of the pre-dawn languor as an orgy draws to an end. The dance flows smoothly through the different parts of the stage, slowly cutting across the space from wing to wing. Everything is numb and just about dead in the ritual tango movements and elegant, ceremonial postures belonging to a world of silvery foliage where the butterflies of twilight are beating their wings in farewell. All seems to be being dispelled into nothingness, demonstrating only the style and form from which life emerged.

There on the square and by the seaside are the bright, simple, well-defined lines of sports suits. There is a blinding white color to blend with red, the color of the sun and victory, or blue, the color of the sky, sea and hopes. Here in the cabaret one meets an affected, decadent style. Gold, yellow and black later turn into an ashen gray-black tone. The decor and rhythm are about the luxury of fading autumn, of a vain but sought astringency.

There in the world of youth we see openness, space, beckoning expanses, life in motion. There we see holidays and workdays; labor and love; art and sport. Here in "The Golden Age" life is all show, vain and empty. An esthetically closed-in world. Here genuine life is feared and everything happening is like a spectacle where there is self-deceit. Here there is an atmosphere of refined beauty where the storms of life have been neglected and run away from. A life failing in its decadence.

The street holiday and the mirth of the restaurant (night, duality of daydreams and duality of existence). In such comparisons there emerges the symbolic depth and exquisiteness of the setting. But here too in the nocturnal shadow of a sheltered lifestyle is the definite aura of the time—in the dresses fashionable in the Twenties and the affected colors of hats, fans and egret-plumes. The decorative and picturesque mise-en-scenes of couples sitting at tables remind one of the illustrated magazines and postcards of the Twenties showing mortal beauties and mortal passions. They are reminiscent of the silent movies. And in that restaurant nightlife the whole atmosphere of that famous New Economic Policy period is captured. The nightclub is enveloped in an enigmatic languor and enwebbed in sudden changes.

The "Golden Age" theme is one of contrasts. Unexpectedly, a further aspect appears, the inner room . . . The restaurant tables, old-style lanterns and dressed-up clients all swim away . . . Amid the gloom we see into the area of the club that is behind the scenes. Suspicious characters, glancing about them as they go, vanish in there in their cocked caps, jackets over tee-shirts, and flamboyant trousers. Another layer of life emerges, one mockingly matted and rollicking. The choreographer presents it in dance-moderne and character dancing.

Wild foot-tapping brings the dance in a whirl of energy to a tornadoing finish . . . The gangsters dance. Using "The Golden Age" as a cover, they get in by a back entrance. Human dignity at the club is measured in terms of evening dress . . . Adorned in a frock coat, the gangster passes for one of the elite. The gang do what they like at "The Golden Age:" lure people to rob, entertain the clients and deceive them. First they earn money from them and then they steal from them.

In the gangster theater all is covered in masks of smiles, overt kindliness and a kind of joyful gameness. But behind the scenes is a robbers' den and the purpose is one: to grab as much as possible and any way possible. The theater has its heroes in Monsieur Jacques (really Yashka) and his comic antagonist, the Master of Ceremonies. The Master of Ceremonies is surrounded by the showgirls who represent the cynical money-buys-all world. The corps-de-ballet has its luminary fooling to the amusement of the crowd and is disdained by it; but he is ready to do anything as a paid service. He covers for the gang while they get on with their dirty business. The character of the gangsters is also shown in large mass scenes, more and more detail added.

We see the gang at leisure, an uncouth, crude mob cowering before the boss, Yashka. He sets the tone in their conjoined dance. His bravura drives his subordinates on, says "this is the way to do things," teaches them foulness and cunning. One moment he is performing innocent, foolish leaps, and then comes a prehensile jump with a firm landing, a shot out of the blue. The gang is delighted and follows the example. Then, devilishly merry, they rob the drunken clients. In another dance episode the Mafia contemplates a big "job." The dance comes out like a plan of action. First there is a vile attack, then people fall to the ground, crawl cautiously and make for some goal . . . Those plastic elements are to then develop into scenes of attack and a chase. Yashka leads in a cavalier manner, rousing the basest instincts, a craving for money. The actual raid is frightfully and cruelly merry. And rollicking then are the celebrations following success, a coarse, cynical display of longing for a sweet life. Languid elements of a tango are woven in.

Each episode throws light forward to the next and deepens the sense. Overall, the choreography is analytical. The thieving gains a symbolic as well as the ordinary mundane sense. It is shown as the focus of immorality, as the deft mask of time-serving people. It is a false lifestyle incarnate; we see the crass hypocrisy of people outwardly smiling and inwardly preparing to stab in the back. Such people lie, betray, and steal from their own sort and others alike, all for their own egoistic interests. Larceny is a sign of moral and spiritual degradation, the result of wild individualist tendencies.

Weaving together the themes of variety and the Mafia, Grigorovich creates plastic action on a scale unheard of. The ambiguous image in "The Golden Age," without losing its spectator value, acquires ominous features.

The main events in the ballet come in key scenes. Coming onto the surface, the plot specifies certain features in the overall picture, shows up details and sharpens the image . . . At times we get just a brief addition to the plot.

Against a background of the merriment in the restaurant, Monsieur Jacques appears for a moment. The club owner and top dancer circles the couples in anxiety and is clearly waiting for someone . . .

Out front comes Rita, the prima donna, in great leaps . . . And the merriment bubbles and fizzes . . . Later, with further turns in the common destiny, we see the sense of these short appearances of the major characters.

The action develops here in dynamic splashes of dance, moved by comparisons and contrasts, attraction and rejection of the various dance impulses.

The events are not described by the choreographer in mundane details. Each happening has a symbolic significance revealed in complex choreographic structures of multi-level dance action.

. . . Fisherman Boris comes to the variety club to search out the unknown young woman who had so captivated him at the festivities in the square. Grigorovich here sets some milestones in the plot and brings various elements into contact. There arises the pure choreographic and theatrical theme of opposition. A white figure (Boris in sports attire) amid the luxury of the restaurant, a clear contour amid pretentious decoration, and straight clear lines of dance as against an affected style. An alien creature for "The Golden Age." Battle begins, covertly and subtly controlled by the gangsters.

In the successive waltzes, charlestons and gallops, as though unintentionally but insistently and vigorously they crowd out the white figure, dividing him from his partner and the others and gradually shutting him out. And a frightened public is involved in that struggle. In the very dancing we see how that world, conservatively closed in on itself, wants nothing to do with the new ways it fears. For the new lifestyle spells a threat to its existence. Though the "renegade" is not openly menaced, a concealed battle is on against him. Finally the intruder is cornered and, fully in keeping with the rules of the gang, is hit in the back and tripped up. All form ranks before Boris; a veritable live bastion bristles. The pause is long and troubled . . . A fragile female hand (Rita) stops the grappling that is due to break out. And the evil bastion parts, the pairs dispel, circling Boris with haughty contempt, studying him watchfully.

"The Golden Age" operates secretly and in that is dangerous. The fight is inevitable but not for the show halls. It's not the right place. Under cover of night the bandits go out on a "job." Robbery or sabotage? No need for definition for we are not talking of a particular crime but of the phenomenon as a whole. A cruel, rogue force has come out to destroy and damage, to impede normal life where only it can. The criminal force of darkness is opposing light. Hence the clashes of the dance and theatrical elements in the ballet.

The plot is built on unexpected happenings and that affords a captivating tension to the action. But these unexpected events show that there are irreconcilable forces and their hostility becomes more and more obvious each time we see them.

Boris came to the variety club by chance. And coincidentally he and his fishermen friends came upon the bandits on the seashore and engaged them in a fight (Act Two). Then there is the chase scene. The whirlwind dance fugue where one set of forces grows, then another, cross, part and come together again . . . We witness a feverish chase where one set loses the other, then catches up. There is hiding and covering over of trails. There is guesswork as to the opponents' next move . . . And here the inner essence of the struggling sides is revealed. One represents wrong, cowardice, and greed. They roll about the ground, clutching to them the loot, leap up in disarray, and, looking around for cover, are once more caught up in a group by their leader.

The other force is assuredly in union, open, free. And once again as events take off the choreographer calls a halt. The fight is not at all simple as embodied in the image of the chase. The gangsters get away. Later the fishermen will again find the tracks of the gang and in Act Three we will see them burst into the secret lair. A short flash of violent action—rhythmic cadence built on acrobatics and karate. The gangsters are surrounded and disarmed. Then we get what seem like two finales: the end of the variety show and the festivities in the square.

These scenes, though evoked by the plot, are not directly linked with it. In the square, Life is celebrating and not just those who expose "The Golden Age." Not all in the restaurant were bandits. Out on the square we see people expressing what is close to their souls. The fishermen are rejoicing at catching the gang and that joy blends into general festive proceedings. The end of that gang spells the downfall of a whole phenomenon.

The final scenes come out of the development of plastic symphony. The sense of the two finales is symbolic. The last restaurant scene comes out as a mad orgy as that way of life realizes it is doomed. The immensity of the Bolshoi Theater stage opens up in all its depth and all the details signifying the place of the events disappear: before us we find a dark, starless, bottomless universe. In front of that abyss people make merry ecstatically and convulsively. The acrobatics of the Master of Ceremonies who then dashes away, the fox-trotting couples 'round about, and the showgirls in the middle mechanically raising their legs all represent a world in panic galloping about the crumbled remains of its former magnificence. A world coming apart and perishing. All rush in a circle which breaks up to scatter them into an endless darkness where they are lost. A mechanism where suddenly all the parts act against each other to destroy the whole.

What has outlived itself departs into nothingness. Instead we find the sun coming up on a new lifestyle. With the end of the restaurant, we get the duet dance of Rita and Boris who affirm love as the infinite source of life. Again the festivities in the square flare brightly as it is filled with young folk. There is a radiant finish to the performance.

Grigorovich's choreography is a marvel. We have the symbolic yet invisible figure of Time which flies pitilessly over life, changing the outmoded with the new. So ends "The Golden Age:" the curtain is descending but the dance continues on stage, the movement never ending.

Love

"The Golden Age" is a real large-scale ballet. What a lot of themes if has, big and small, all fused into one! Showing in contrasts and comparisons the various dance elements, the choreographer indicates generally the multitude of live phenomena: different lifestyles and modes of existence, diverse views on the world and diverse approaches to actual living. The adventurous plot deepens the contrasts. But from the mass scenes Grigorovich passes to the more personal, from the social atmosphere of the era to the theme of the value of each human being, its beauty and uniqueness. The ballet is made the more poetic and soulful by the interest in the human heart and mind, by the belief in human dignity. The march beats are softened by warmth of soul.

The 1930 scenario gave Shostakovich no chance to embody his lyrical ideas but the composer had a will of his own and in individual episodes broke through. The modern version has picked them out. The lyrical dances of the young women and fishermen by the shore are to the music of the original score. It also contained the music on which the first duet of Rita and Boris and one of Rita's variations are based.

That lyrical beginning produced by Shostakovich was developed by Grigorovich who took the theme of love through the whole performance. Love, that most elevated human emotion, the one that breeds life and for which good deeds are done. The theme, as has been mentioned comes out in the mass dances by the sea but it acquires true depth in four major adagios performed by the hero and heroine. Here we have the first chance meeting and the joking play of acquaintance. And there are doubts and fears . . . Tender recognition and flight of emotion developing into the height of passion. These adagios, always with our heroes alone and without the corps-de-ballet, go right to the center of the heart, touch the finest strings of the soul and reveal the most secret emotions. These four episodes tell an entire love story.

The duets are also about a general image of good, purity and humanity. Linked in terms of drama and choreography with the mass scenes displaying the new lifestyle, they pierce deeper into the fabric of that new mode of living and form the moral focus of it.

In some cases the duets come straight after dance showing the new reality: amid the general throng we are given a specific example. In Act One, for instance, Boris and Rita first glimpse each other as the general festivities draw to a conclusion. They dance a duet to seal their meeting. At the end of the work scene (Act Two) Rita comes looking for Boris and again they duet. In the remaining instances, the heroes meet after conflict situations: after Boris clashes with Yashka in the club, and when the variety facade collapses as the fishermen break up the gang. After these more violent moments the duets give us a more profound realization of events. Following the heat of struggle, we find harmony as the action returns to more natural human sentiments.

Each of the three acts notably finishes with a lyrical theme. The first act concludes with a major duet dance which comes in a special two parts. It begins amid the restaurant decorations (after Yashka and Boris clash). The hero and heroine are together but each seems to be looking deep to his own thoughts and feelings, considering what has happened and checking himself and his plans, hopes, and dreams. In the second half the props gradually disappear to leave a limitless expanse. And love is spoken of in reverent, quivering movements full of tenderness and poetry. The two are both a part of the world and all the world. Love triumphs throughout the Universe. In such a romantic and victorious mood ends Act One.

The finale of Act Two has lyrics otherwise expressed in short but dramatic and impassioned cadence. Boris, trussed up by the gangsters. is saved and the couple is reunited. Rita and Boris fly towards each other, borne up high by converging groups of the corps-de-ballet.

The very last scene of the ballet contains a wildly glad lyrical chord. Holding her high above the rejoicing throng, Boris whirls Rita.

The choreography of these duets is intriguing. Starting off on the ground, the duets gain more and more upper holds. High surges are the leitmotif of Rita's part and are quite a few of them in her restaurant dances. But there the flights are effectively accentuated. In the lyrical adagios the holds are interpreted unconventionally: Grigorovich applies to them the principle of cantilena which is inherently par terre, while dance periods are created in the air which flow smoothly one into another. In the air an azure picture is painted, like the top of an exotic tree: it leafs, blossoms and disappears into the sky. The heroine is whirled in the hands of the hero and he spins along with her. And those circles seemingly diverging, the movement covers the whole immense area of the stage. Hence the spinning of life and the circulation of the heart are joined to the lyrical message.

The love line, according to the plot, also has its detective side. The sparkling showbird falls in love unexpectedly, but really, with a simple fellow. And on the contrary, the demonstrable love of Yashka for Lyuska collapses. Furtively Yashka is seeking the affections of Rita, and Lyuska discovers this. The duets of Yashka and Rita as a couple are always in public places, either in the restaurant hall or amid the gang. This is questionable love reflecting a cynical morality which says one thing and does quite another.

The walls of "The Golden Age" stand for deception and hypocrisy. The victims relentlessly change places in an effort to outdo each other in despicable things. Act One shows Lyuska enticing two drunken clients to be robbed, and one is strangled by her friends. And later, in Act Three, she herself perishes in a violent scene of envy. The detective events lead to tragedy.

Yuri
Vasyuchenko
as Boris

Natalya Bessmertnova as Rita

Chapter 3

A Ballet of Unexpected Discoveries

This ballet dramatically produces many unexpected things. Grigorovich, the renowned choreographer, a philosopher and romantic, creates an effective detective story and is shown to have a clear gift for parody and to have sparkling humor. The veteran ballet-master comes out bright, cheerful and very young. And not because the ballet is about young people. Rather because the master who made it is brimming with fine ideas and spends his strength willingly, surmounting all difficulty. Fantasy and innovation race side by side. This ballet is all about flight of imagination; the limitless art in it is truly Mozartian. Composer and choreographer enjoy a oneness born over years of joint creativity. Grigorovich has brought back to the theater the Shostakovich named by Glazunov at the time of his First Symphony and first ballet as "our Mozart."

"The Golden Age" discovers unexpected frontiers in the talented players. Isn't it a surprise to see the incomparable romantic ballerina Natalya Bessmertnova suddenly in the role of showgirl? A flighty, cantilena dancer who produces a tango with acrobatics. The role of Rita is considered one of Bessmertnova's greatest.

Not that the ballerina rejects her former self. She transforms in a most magic way both the romantic theme in her art and the face of her dancing.

Bessmertnova's Rita is a good person who has ended up by some fluke at the "The Golden Age" cabaret club. She is out of place there but somehow works there.

The dancing of the ballerina, without losing any of its precision, has acquired a fine acerbity. The idol of "The Golden Age," her Rita lights up her audience. She is elegantly audacious, aristocratically effective and captivates the public with mind-boggling acrobatics switching into effortless turns and spins . . . The star dances her tango with bravura and gay dignity. She finds real art and climbs above the everyday atmosphere to attain true beauty. She achieves a golden age of her own which has nothing to do with the sordid, hypocritical and bubbly nightclub . . .

Bessmertnova in the role of Rita creates an image where terrestrial sensitivity, luring availability and aristocratic aloofness all combine. The heroine seems to have a supernatural quality: one touch and the image fades . . .

As Rita, Bessmertnova catches not the Sylphide, airy romantic theme but the most cardinal: the life of the performer with all the complex, dual artistic conscience and the constant battle within the soul. For this Rita the theater is a delighted prisoner languishing in its closed character but attracts with the mighty and magic power of beauty. Bessmertnova's Rita, like a true artist, thirsts to escape, to get away from that theater but to eventually get back to her proper calling.

From the limited world of art she makes for freedom, for the spontaneity of natural life with its unexpected turns, for the big world to which the eternal will of the artist and player calls her forcefully. Outside the walls of "The Golden Age" she revels in the taste of freedom. The plastic culmination of her duets and variations lies in a broad flightfulness where the dance soars. On the variety stage Rita is alluring, and now she too is tempted in actual life, something she reacts to with lively curiosity and touching timidity.

Shyly glad, she joins Boris's circle of friends and dances with them, catching on quickly to their style and adopting some things from them to apply in her own dance. A thirst for the unknown and unexplored attracts her to a simple fellow with extraordinary character. And again come the spiritual struggles, the desire for love and constant trial of feelings. The love duets of the heroine are filled with latently elegaic, deeply tender and passionate movements from the soul. Art and life, finesses and naturalness fuse into one. A brilliant example of this is provided by the dancing of Bessmertnova.

Tatyana Golikova is likewise a surprise in the role of Lyuska. She is an experienced ballerina noted for her versatility. She has played the fairy-tale parts Odetta-Odillia, and fairy Syreny, as well as the tragic queen Mekhmene Banu in Grigorovich's version of "Legend of Love," and the courtesan Egina in his stage version of "Spartacus" . . . But Lyuska is quite a new departure. Those others were roles involving mostly classical dance. This role is all about character dancing, though the character dance here gets up on its toes.

Golikova is brilliant in the new role. She gets right inside an unconventional genre. Paradoxically her dancing blends parody and grotesquerie with a daintiness that makes the image complex and significant. Each and every affected or lisping and flirty step has its own special grace and tenderness but the whole is presented with sovereign disdain. Her dances behind the wings among her own type are mocking and contemptuous. She fools about disdainfully as though purely for the hell of it. Exaggerated and grotesque movements show the style, manner, and breed.

The heroine played by Golikova is far from the countess who has descended into gangster company and hit rock bottom. This is a lost soul that has tragically outlived itself and has found such a warped method of avenging for a life that had not taken place. Lyuska has the self-possession of a lady of high society and she does not face by open expression of her feelings. But behind the mask, Golikova's heroine is alight with hate and that hate flames up when the time comes for the really big job. Here Lyuska is feverishly active, inciting Yashka and driving him on. She is no mere accomplice taking orders but an inspirer, an evil genius, a partner equal in intelligence, craft, and ruthlessness. Lyuska deep down does not experience love for Yashka. Her embraces and tender gestures are presented as a game to play with. But Yashka is a support in avenging a hated world. Hence he is not indifferent. Thus the fierceness of the finale: the envy is not for the rival but for the "business" which may fall through due to the frivolity of the owner.

The choice of performers is made by Grigorovich over and over again and always according to a fixed pattern: the genuine talent and the current form of the players. Bessmertnova is today the undisputed prima donna of the Bolshoi Ballet. Golikova is a leading ballerina who had made a name for herself before "The Golden Age." But for the same roles Grigorovich has also chosen younger people: Alla Mikhalchenko (Rita) and Maria Bylova (Lyuska), who both joined the company in the late Seventies. The balletmaster went through the roles at the one time with experienced and novices alike, and put both sets into première performances at the same time, affording the young a chance to show their worth. The trust of the choreographer proved justified and this brought out the richness of his choreography the more, for in these roles the new performers found their own shades and placed their own accents.

Mikhalchenko as Rita highlighted the theme of the soul being roused to form character. She seems to have two parts to the role which are developed in psychological continuity. First there is a pacific frame of mind whereby a person is self-satisfied and knows no doubts or anxieties. Her Rita lives theater and dreams theater without noticing the tawdriness and hollowness of the glittering cabaret. She reigns supreme on that stage and triumphantly sees herself as a show personality. In the festive square she seems to improvise for herself a new role as a simple young woman: she mixes stylish grandeur with naive simplicity. The duet of acquaintance which she dances with Boris is an exquisite and flirtatious parody of the prima donna in an exotic "novel." The episodes are arranged as the fantasies of an actress measuring up for herself different roles, and the passivity here far from signifies monotony.

The first part of the role demonstrates the artistry of nature, the second—the humanity of soul. The theatrical vicious circle is broken by the

Tatyana Golikova as Lyuska

whirlwind events of life which require actions and a choice. The first act is when Rita stops the row in the restaurant. For the heroine played by Alla Mikhalchenko this is an involuntary impulse she had not expected of herself and this brings her to perturbation and reflection. The further development of the role is a forceful emotional crescendo. Each dance represents an act that frees more and more strength of soul and represents valor, resolve, tenderness, and passion . . . Rita does not betray her vocation as a player. Among Boris's friends she dances not so much with them as for them, making every step effective. But she is oblivious of the attraction to a new way of life and new public which open up before her along with love.

And in the role of Lyuska alongside Golikova Maria Bylova is also a revelation. A dancer of classical parts who was the beautiful Queen of Driads in "Don Quixote" and "Florina" in "The Sleeping Beauty," she was considered pre-ordained for such parts where all-important is the sphere of "pure" dance, and fanciful images far from earthly feelings. The role of Lyuska (the first leading role for the young player in a major ballet) revealed in her a ballerina of bubbling temperament capable of good sharp contrasts in her dancing.

For this Lyuska all is hyperbolized. In the cabaret parlor she is the picture of good manners, languidity and sweetness. In the gang she stands for energy, force and ruthlessness. In all she has a tough bravura. This Lyuska lives fast and is determined to grab from life anything that's going.

She is desperately gay in the restaurant, her languidly bashful dance exploding into sharp accents, stunning a venerable public and deceiving. Her changes of partner are abrupt and instantaneous. As though latching onto their mood, she hastens to fire the passion in each of them. She defiantly shows off to the gangsters. She is their equal and can even do better than they. And she participates in the raids with predatory fervor. Bylova's Lyuska is reckless, a fast-liver, someone who loves extreme sensations. A type of anarchist who wants a pretty lifestyle with plenty of money. But that image bears dramatism. The cynical Lyuska sentimentally loves Yashka, notices his every look and gesture. For him she would do anything. Was it perhaps love that brought this foolhardy creature to the gang? That switched her from the straight path and ruined her?

With the first ballet, Sergei Prokofiev's "The Stone Flower" back in 1957, Grigorovich put on the stage a whole new generation of ballet artists and determined a new style of dancing which made the destiny of his leading dancers. Later, in 1968 and Aram Khachaturian's "Spartacus," Grigorovich opened the road before a further generation. And so it was with "The Golden Age" too. Grigorovich was true to his principle of giving the young a chance and presented the new stars of the Eighties. He has young people in the corps-de-ballet, solo episodes and leading roles. The major men's parts are all performed by young people.

Thus, the ballet itself affirmed the maturity of the new generation and brought forth a new galaxy of stars.

I have mentioned the ladies but the men were no less sensational. Going out alongside the unique Bessmertnova, Irek Mukhamedov with the role of Boris asserted himself as the Bolshoi's top male performer. Up to then the highest standard of male dancing was the role of "Spartacus" as played by Vasiliev. The role of Boris surpassed that phenomenal achievement. The part was designed specially for the tremendous ability of Mukhamedov. The young man had already played Spartacus astoundingly at just 21. For all its depth of talent, the Bolshoi had never known so young a Spartacus. It was Mukhamedov's first work with the company which he came to straight after a Grand Prix at the Moscow International Competition in 1981.

That Competition victory upset the pundits. An unknown graduate of the Moscow Choreographic School, he didn't figure in the experts' forecasts. But round by round he impressed audiences and jury alike. In the third and final round he received such an ovation for his rendering of the pas-de-deux from "Don Quixote" that the Bolshoi's famous chandelier must have been in risk of cracking.

"He confounded us," Grigorovich, the chairman of the jury, confessed afterward. Mukhamedov was immediately invited to join the Bolshoi and in just three months mastered the part of Spartacus, something that had taken an experienced Vasiliev half a year.

The part of Boris, though, was the first specially made for him. His Boris is robust and a born leader. He has chosen his way in life and proceeded unerringly along it. He develops here the heroic theme embodying the pathetically elevated beauty of the leading lady. His performance is a hymn sung of the heroes, of an ardently pure faith in life as something wonderful, in people as great. Mukhamedov's Boris is ever in the air. His dancing needs no dramatic decor; it materializes as a symbol of the aspirations of the human soul to go up, up and away, to reach for the stars. Such is the unbelievable airiness of Mukhamedov's performance, so expressive is his fervent energy, so beautiful his springy rhythm.

He does impossible virtuoso combinations. And the pace he sets himself is incredible, growing to hurricane force by the end of the ballet. It's hard for the naked eye to keep up with him . . . And, as photography confirms, there is absolute pureness of movement at any given moment. That is also probably a secret behind the exemplary power of his dancing, the sculptured lines and whirlwind finish. This dancing is concentrated and devoid of all bravado. It does not stop at mastery and effects. It comes across symbolically as a specter, a generalized image. In it the ideal has the upper hand; the noble idea comes first. It contains thrust to immortal beauty and infinite perfection.

It is self-evident that Boris has the ability to drive people on as they fight

Irek Mukhamedov as Boris

the enemy, work, and sail dangerous seas. He is the best athlete and the top player in their theater. This fiery dancer has an infectious sense of humor and wittily parodies the tsarist general in the political theater production. And his lyrics are outstanding in the duet dances of love. This is the love of Romeo: at first sight and for ever. It contains knightly effusiveness which with every new meeting finds more and more beauty in the beloved. Each time he sees her, this Boris elevates his Rita still higher and bows lower and lower to her. Precisely such a hero reaching out for all that is fine was needed to capture and fulfill the refined heroine played by Bessmertnova.

The same holds for the other leading pair. The success-spoiled prima donna played by Mikhalchenko would attract the touchingly simple-hearted, trusting and open Boris as acted by Yuri Vasyuchenko. He takes a different line from Mukhamedov: discovery of life, a maturing of spirit and how people become heroes.

That Boris accepts the life opening up before him no less unhesitatingly than the first. He tries his strength in a naive and pure exultation—but he is only starting out in life and all seems radiant. He is not yet ready for adversity. Every mean trick catches him unaware and he suffers terribly. He is shocked and pained but invariably hopeful. Vasyuchenko's dancing is most emotional and breezily expresses the multitude of nuances to contradicting feelings.

Mukhamedov's Boris shoots like an arrow about "The Golden Age" club, not wasting time to look at the clientele. Self-assured, he is not bothered by their coldness and disregard. Vasyuchenko's Boris is curious, indignant and alarmed . . . The meeting with Rita is not only happy but determines his salvation. His perturbation makes the cabaret prima donna want to encourage him, and it originally evokes her indulgent care and tenderness.

The love song of this Boris begins with shy avowals and doubts as to whether love is possible. His feelings gradually grow stronger and bolder. And Vasyuchenko's dancing flows in pretty and protracted lines and exaltation. His soul is released from shyness and attains a proud resolution and passionate dedication. Inside the lyrical and soft-centered Boris, a warrior awakens who not only rallies to the new way of life but stands up in its defense and for his love.

Vasyuchenko, a dancer of the lyrical and romantic make-up most exalted prior in the character of Siegfried in "The Swan Lake," has now revealed the more heroic qualities of his talent. The maturing of a man is the heart of his interpretation and has proved a happy image and fact in the biography of the young performer himself. Precisely in "The Golden Age" he attained a stable virtuosity and assured mastery.

Talent and individuality are sensed by Grigorovich with pinpoint accuracy. He sees things nobody else does. Hence his amazing knack for blending performers. "The Golden Age" is rich in surprise choices of dancers. Per-

Yuri Grigorovich rehearsing with the young dancers of the Bolshoi.

haps the greatest surprise is Gediminas Taranda in the role of Yashka. In him a new star was discovered from the ranks of the unknown. In his second year of work at the Theater, Taranda was given this difficult leading role. Before that he had danced but a few episode roles and those who saw him did not notice anything special. Grigorovich recognized the extent of the talent and brought him into his new ballet from the start, and into the first group where he would partner famous ballerinas. The première made him a star.

Taranda's interpretation is attractive and unconventional for a villain's role. He performs the giddy tango with aristocratic ease. The ecstasy of the audience is received by him with gratified modesty. Everyone gets a smile and consideration. He seems to love one and all. That elegant, charming and cheery performer is all charisma. He bewitches like the best of magicians, and contrives to gain people's trust. He craftily weaves intrigue before everyone's very eyes but no one sees it. A seemingly casual turn of the head and once again he is engrossed in the dance and his partner. But the secret signal has been conveyed to his accomplices and they are planning their dirty deeds against chosen victims. And he appears to have nothing to do with it.

He is just as carefree among the gang. His plastic, light and flexible dancing is an original tale of his ill doings . . . He presents it all as a gay adventure after which he ends up with neat profit in his pocket . . . Then off he goes, charming again. He has a good sense of his colleagues' apprehensions and fears and relates ironically to the gang as people of low intellect.

Taranda's Yashka is a game character who enjoys the element of risk and has a desperate passion to always be in the thick of things. He demands love from Rita as proof of his own irresistibility. He takes similar pleasure from the big raid and the petty theft. He would stop at nothing and would kill for anything. He cynically juggles with the cue just used to strangle a man and that same murderous hand is gallantly presented, all smiles, to a lady, inviting her to waltz.

Taranda is the quintessence of an individualist outlook. A person socially dangerous and a diehard with complete and utter atrophy of moral and spiritual values. He is the sort who cold-bloodedly betrays and robs other people and his own alike and those he serves on a pathological principle of taking most for himself. For egoistic gain he would ruthlessly do anything.

The plasticity of the role is as follows: a carefree and smiling light-heartedness and for a brief moment, discipline, a pounce, and a predatory and reckless grab. "Murder with a smile" would seem to be his terrible motto. The picture is deeply theatrical and the young dancer portrays excellently the deceptive outer appearance and dangerous mirages.

The difference between the images created by the dancers in the same roles is the more striking if one considers that the two sets of performers rehearsed at about the same time. Each found his own thing and each work is bright, which is an indication of the talent of the company and of the depth of the script and choreography.

Yashka's role also had another performer, Alexei Lazarev. His Yashka is cruel, scheming and secretive. A businessman in the past, he now has to adapt to new conditions. But he has not lost his superior bearing. He's a boss and used to being obeyed, whether in the restaurant or among the gangsters. On stage he is correctness itself, irreproachably precise and strict. No pleasure for himself. He demonstrates manners and vogue . . . He does his bit, "producing the goods," only condescendingly, with no flirtation but rather with cool courtesy. There is alarming pent-up energy. We get a sense of the quiet before the storm.

And that storm breaks behind the wings, a storm of long concealed feelings that is exceptionally fierce and breeds gloomy ideas and designs . . . He aspires to crumble and destroy a lifestyle that has dropped him overboard and made him wriggle. The main theme in Taranda's dance is impetuosity; for Lazarev it is a sinister force that presses and bites. With the same menacing authority he orders his men to robbery or battle. Love is nothing lasting for him, just momentary amusement to get away from frenetic thinking. For this Yashka, Lyuska is a nobody vainly hoping for more. And Rita? Not implicated, she jeopardizes the cause. So she has to be subjugated by some means or other. Thus Lazarev builds the role of Yashka which has become a landmark in his career. His dancing is virtuoso, fervent and attractive. In "The Golden Age" he shows artistic control over an uncommon temperament. An actor who had significant accomplishments before, he achieved real mastery with this role.

Nearly all the performers in "The Golden Age" are graduates of the Moscow Choreographic School directed by Sophia Golovkina. Alla Mikhalchenko was a pupil of hers. Of the leading players only Yuri Vasyuchenko comes from Leningrad. But for some reason he left that city after school and went to Alma-Ata, the capital of Kazakhstan. He came to the All-Union Ballet Competition from there in 1980 which he won and was invited by Grigorovich to join the Bolshoi Theater. Now he parallels Mukhamedov (a friend) in dancing the entire repertoire of the Company.

Since the première, other performers have appeared in "The Golden Age." They include Andris Liepa (Boris), the son of Maris Liepa who was once a solo dancer with the Bolshoi Ballet and performed famously the role of Crassus in Grigorovich's version of "Spartacus."

The newcomers also include the illustrious Lyudmila Semenyaka, who debuted as Rita during a Paris tour, and Nina Semizorova who debuted as Lyuska when the Bolshoi Ballet Company visited London.

International Acclaim

Moscow in March 1983 saw an International Ballet Seminar in whch choreographers, teachers and ballet experts from twenty countries participated. In the evenings they watched performances by the Bolshoi Ballet Theater and by day discussed what they had seen and common issues related to development of choreography as an art.

The Bolshoi Theater put on ten ballet versions by as many contemporary Soviet ballet-masters. All of them were well received but the success of "The Golden Age" stood out on its own. When Grigorovich appeared in the conference hall the morning after the ballet was performed, he received a real ovation. And in the course of the debate there was unanimous recognition that "The Golden Age" was a new word in choreography. This was a first international success.

In the years 1984-86 the Bolshoi Ballet then performed "The Golden Age" while on tour in West Germany, Austria, Britain, France, Argentina and Brazil. Everywhere the public was enthusiastic and the press had words of praise. In the famous Covent Garden theater in London, "The Golden Age" was shown six times in six weeks. In the Palais de Congres in Paris it was performed fifteen times in a month, nine times in succession to start. These figures speak for themselves.

The newspaper 'Jours de France' wrote: " . . . now the Russians have a West Side Story all their own." Jacques Puissy, the Director of the Comédie Française, congratulated the Bolshoi Company on their triumph and said: "Until this evening, I had no idea that ballet possessed such great opportunities." 'Le Monde' headed its review "A Performance That Invariably Charms." 'L 'Humanité said: " . . . the most distinctive feature of Grigorovich is an ability to express in dance of incredible richness the action, characters and even the thoughts of the players. The supreme example of this is provided by his choreographic presentation of 'The Golden Age'."

Grigorovich brought three bulky volumes of reviews home from the tour to Britain. Some magazines and papers even wrote about 'The Golden Age' several times as different performers brought out new, unfathomed details in the dance. The eminent Clement Crisp said in the 'Financial Times' that Grigorovich had put on a ballet giving an extraordinarily strong picture of a young state setting about forming a future for itself. He continued that Grigorovich had also presented a picture of his own company which just stunned one with its growth and pulsating energy. All this, says Crisp, fuses into a superb theatrical exhibition.

'The Observer' noted that the ballet had given "the greatest of pleasure." The 'Birmingham Post' echoed that idea, saying that 'The Golden Age' gave the audience the broadest of ranges of enjoyment.

We could go on quoting infinitely for 'The Golden Age' has clearly made it internationally. Now, in 1987 Yuri Grigorovich is working on the second Shostakovich ballet, 'The Bolt.'

Designer Simon Virsaladze in a discussion with Yuri Grigorovich.

ГОСУДАРСТВЕННЫЙ АКАДЕМИЧЕСКИЙ БОЛЬШОЙ ТЕАТР С

ШОСТАКОВИЧ ДМИТР

БАЛЕТ В 3^х ДЕЙСТВИЯХ

ЗОЛОТОЙ ВЕК

ХОРЕОГРАФИЯ ЮРИЯ ГРИГОРОВИЧА

poster of "The Golden Age" performance.

INFORMATION ABOUT THE COLOR PHOTOGRAPHS

pg. 57 A Youth Festivity. Act 1
pg. 58 Yuri Vasuychenko as Boris
pg. 59 Andris Liepa as Boris
pg. 61 Irek Mukhamedov as Boris
pg.62-63 A Youth Theatre Performance. Act 1
pg. 64 Alla Mikhalchenko as Rita
pg. 65 Natalya Bessmertnova as Rita; Irek Mukhamedov as Boris
pg. 66 Nina Semizorova as Lyuska with Yuri Vetrov and Vladimir Elagin
pg. 67 Tatyana Golikova as Lyuska with Yuri Vetrov and Mikhail Meneyv
pg.68-69 Murder of a drunk bourgeois backstage of "The Golden Age" cabaret
pg. 70 Mikhail Tzivin as Master of Ceremonies at "The Golden Age"
pg. 71 Stanislav Chasov as Master of Ceremonies at "The Golden Age"
pg. 72 Natalya Bessmertnova as Rita
pg. 73-75 Natalya Bessmertnova as Rita; Gediminas Taranda as Monsieur Jacques
pg.76-77 Natalya Bessmertnova as Rita; Yuri Vasyuchenko as Boris; Tatyana Golikova as Lyuska; Gediminas Taranda as Monsieur Jacques
pg. 78 Lyudmila Semenyaka as Rita; Andris Liepa as Boris
pg. 79 Alla Mikhalchenko as Rita; Irek Mukhamedov as Boris
pg. 80-81 Natalya Bessmertnova as Rita; Irek Mukhamedov as Boris
pg.82-83 "The Golden Age" restaurant in the night hours. Act 2
pg. 84 Mikhail Tzivin as Master of Ceremonies at "The Golden Age"
pg. 85 Alla Mikhalchenko as Rita; Gediminas Taranda as Monsieur Jacques
pg. 87 Yashka's gang of bandits fleeing with their loot. Act 2
pg.88-89 Young fishermen led by Boris. Act 2
pg.90-91 Fishermen are off to the high seas while their girls stay on shore awaiting their return. Act 2
pg. 92 Alla Mikhalchenko as Rita; Irek Mukhamedov as Boris
pg. 93 Natalya Bessmertnova as Rita
pg. 94 Irek Mukhamedov as Boris
pg. 95-98 Natalya Bessmertnova as Rita; Irek Mukhamedov as Boris
pg. 99 Tatyana Golikova as Lyuska; Gediminas Taranda as Yashka

Synopsis of the Ballet "The Golden Age"

ACT ONE

Scene One — Popular festivities in post-revolutionary Russia. Rita is among the public watching the athletes' parade and the workers' youth theatre performance. Among the most active participants of the festivities is a young fisherman, Boris. Rita and Boris meet, but she vanishes without so much as telling him her name. Boris sets off to look for Rita.

Scene Two — —His search brings Boris to "The Golden Age" nightclub. The show is on. Mademoiselle Margot and Monsieur Jacques are the focus of everybody's attention. Boris is stunned to recognize in Mademoiselle Margot the girl with whom he fell in love. He took her for a working girl (and she surely wanted to pass for one), but she appears to be a flamboyant prima donna of a cabaret... Nevertheless Rita and Boris are both happy to find each other and their mutual joy does not go unnoticed by Monsieur Jacques.

Scene Three — Monsieur Jacques's real name is Yashka, the ringleader of a gang of bandits. Under the pretense of being "The Golden Age" customer, Yashka's girlfriend, Lyuska, lures two drunken "money-bags" from the restaurant to a blind alley to be robbed by her accomplices. One of them fights back and is killed by Yashka.

Scene Four — Returning to the nightclub, Monsieur Jacques finds Rita together with Boris. Consumed with jealousy, he picks a fight with his unexpected rival, but Rita boldly breaks it up separating the two men.

Scene Five — Boris and Rita are finally left alone. Boris confesses his love for her. Never before has Rita been so happy.

ACT TWO

Scene One   Getting Rita alone, Monsieur Jacques demands her love. She rejects him and he becomes more persistent, but Rita runs off to seek Boris's protection.

Scene Two   Yashka conspires and incites his men to another crime. After the robbery the bandits hide away with the loot.

Scene Three   The young fishermen are working by the seashore. There Rita finds Boris. Seeing how warmly his friends welcome her she eagerly joins them. Finally Boris and Rita are alone on the shore. The robbers fleeing from the place of the crime unexpectedly stumble upon them . . . They attack Boris and Rita, the unneeded witnesses, and Boris almost perishes in an unequal combat. Fortunately, Rita manages to break away and run off for help. Boris's friends arrive in time to rescue him from a sure death. The fishermen led by Boris start off in pursuit of the criminals.

ACT THREE

Scene One   Yashka's gang is celebrating in their den. Boris and his friends burst in. Most of the gangsters are captured, but Yashka and Lyuska escape.

Scene Two   The variety show is in full swing. Rita is doing her number with Monsieur Jacques not suspecting that he is the bandits' ringleader. All her thoughts are of Boris. She is revolted by the atmosphere of the cabaret.

Scene Three   Rita resolves to leave "The Golden Age" for good. But Monsieur Jacques bars her way. He insistently seeks her affections. Lyuska happens to witness the scene. Blinded by envy, she hurls herself at Yashka with a knife. Grabbing the knife from Lyuska, he unintentionally stabs her with it.

Scene Four   Being the eye-witness of the murder, Rita is taken captive by the hoodlums who lead her at a knife-point back onto the stage. The fishermen burst into the nightclub in search of Yashka. In the midst of the general panic Yashka tries to run away taking Rita as a hostage, but he is stopped short . . .

Scene Five   The gang of bandits is broken up. Rita and Boris are happily reunited. Their great joy is shared by friends.

In the roaring Twenties of Russia outdoor festivities are very popular. Many different kinds of people are engaged in the animated, bright affairs. There are workers, fishermen, working girls in their red headscarves, kids, sailors, a cigarette girl, and a newspaper boy...
Life itself is bubbling and thriving.

As in many outdoor festivities, there is a parade of athletes. The one who catches everybody's eye in the sporting performance is a fisherman named Boris.

Boris is the most skilled of the athletes. He arouses the admiration of the spectators by his strength and agility.

Young people from all over the town come together to watch the athletes' parade and theatrical performances, to partake of the general merriment and participate in the proletarian manifestation. This is the new generation that is starting out, the youth in the doorway of life with its tantalizing opportunities. And Boris is in the very center of the goings-on. One can immediately feel the leadership in that young man. No wonder he enjoys popularity among his friends, the fishermen.

The athletes in the square are replaced by a youth theatre company. They perform a play mocking the deposed Tsar. A new generation of workers are sweeping their native land clean of tsarist generals, priests, bankers, and all those who were making their fortunes on the sweat of the toiling people.

Curiosity brings Rita, the star of "The Golden Age" variety nightclub, to the square to watch the festivities. Passing off as a working girl she delights in the opportunity to be among the unpretending open-hearted young people, to act freely, just to be herself.

Boris meets Rita and falls in love with her at first sight. When night falls Rita has to return to the nightclub to perform. She vanishes from the square like Cinderella, as unexpectedly and mysteriously as she appeared there.

The lights of "The Golden Age" nightclub beckon the rich... The New Economic Policy introduced in Russia in the Twenties allowed private enterprise which gave rise to a new "elite" class that raised its head for a short period. They seek pleasures in restaurants and variety shows. Heading for "The Golden Age", two businessmen pick up a seductive young lady.

Little do the stupid "money-bags", all prepared to enjoy themselves, suspect that they are trapped by a girl from a gang of bandits who use "The Golden Age" as a cover. Among the brigands the girl is known as Lyuska. Meanwhile she and her new-found admirers make merry at "The Golden Age", where the old lifestyle is having a final swing.

Lyuska lures the two drunken businessmen into a blind alley behind "The Golden Age" building to be robbed by her accomplices. One of the victims appears less drunk than he seemed to be and fights back. Fearing to be recognized by him, the gang leader, Yashka, kills him.

The Master of Ceremonies at "The Golden Age" entertains the public. Here life is all show, vain and empty. It is all hypocrisy and pretense.

To the delight of "The Golden Age" customers, they are treated to a tempting parade of the "girls" led by the feverishly prancing Master of Ceremonies.

The variety show continues. The prize of the night is always the sparkling prima donna Rita. Her number tops the bill. Elegant, gracious and feminine, she fascinates the viewers with her exquisite dancing. As always they welcome her enthusiastically.

Rita and her partner Monsieur Jacques perform an exotic number to the exulted applause of "The Golden Age" patrons.

Dancing with Monsieur Jacques in "The Golden Age", Rita has not the slightest idea that her partner is none other than Yashka, the ringleader of the gang of bandits feared by the whole town.

Having lost sight of Rita in the town square, Boris sets out to find her. His search brings him to "The Golden Age". An alien creature in a decadent cabaret, Boris is looked upon with haughty contempt.

To his great astonishment Boris learns that the girl he has fallen in love with is a "show girl". He is determined to take her away from "The Golden Age". Monsieur Jacques, or Yashka, being jealous of Rita, picks a fight with the stranger who appears to be his rival, but Rita bravely separates the two men.

Rita is ashamed of having tried to deceive Boris by keeping from him she is a show girl...

Rita is further perturbed by the events of the past evening. Boris comforts her. He does not care what her past life was. He is looking forward to a happy future for them together.

The better Rita and Boris get to know each other, the more deeply are they in love.

Rita and Boris never want to part... perhaps for the first time in her life Rita is truly happy.

In "The Golden Age" life is in the throes of a desperate last fling complete with the rousing cancan and the mournful, melancholy, languishing tango "Tahiti Trot".

The Master of Ceremonies arouses the public's passions with his fiery dance.

Alone with Rita, Monsieur Jacques seeks her love. Being rejected by her he becomes ever more insistent in his demands. Rita forcefully resists him.

Yashka is not one for senti-
mentality. He is not used to
taking "No" for an answer.
Meanwhile there is no time to
lose. He casts off his show
clothes to resume the leadership of the gang. After a major
robbery, the bandits run away
with the loot.

Rain or shine, storm or no storm, the brave fishermen are off to work. They show the bold human spirit that has no fears. It is Boris who leads them.

The fishermen's sweethearts see them off to sea
and remain on the shore awaiting their return.

Upset by Monsieur Jacques's vulgar advances and feeling unhappy, Rita comes to the shore looking for Boris to pour out her heart to him.

Seeing how warmly Boris's friends welcome her, Rita gladly joins in their merriment. No matter how hard the fishermen and their girls work, they are always optimistic and full of vigor, never brooding or complaining about their constant dangerous fight against the unpredictable seas.

Only now does Rita fully realize what an extraordinary person is Boris. She is fascinated by his courage.

Boris is a truly romantic hero and it seems to Rita she is unworthy of him, unworthy of his love...

For Rita, Boris is a fine and fearless knight, personifying courage, inspiration and high hopes. Boris really loves her and wants her to forget all about her life as a show girl catering to the tastes of the drunken nightclub clientele.

Rita does not dare believe in her good fortune. It all seems like a dream to her.

Rita feels utterly happy with Boris. She has at last understood what it means to be truly in love and be loved.

Searching for a hiding place for their loot, Yashka and his gang appear on the shore. Seeing Boris and Rita there the hoodlums panic. They want no eye witnesses. Ordering Lyuska to hide before Rita spots her, Yashka dons a mask to disguise himself and tries to get rid of Boris.

Boris puts up a fight, but there are too many bandits for him to overpower. They tie him up and toss him onto the shoreline to be swept off by the waves. In the commotion of the fight Rita fortunately manages to run off for help.

The gang gets away. But Boris's friends are already on the trail. The fishermen rescue Boris from a sure death. Rita and Boris are happily reunited while their friends set off to chase the gang.

The gang celebrates the lucky outcome of their successful venture. They managed to shake off the pursuing fishermen and are now gathered in their den for an orgy.

The gang leader Yashka is pleased with Lyuska's loyalty to him and condescendingly accepts her love and submissiveness.

The gang's hilarious celebration is at
its height...

Lyuska, the ringleader's girl, enjoys being the center of everyone's attention.

Weary of his double life as Monsieur Jacques, Yashka is delighted to be in his own element and lets his violent temper loose. However, it is time for him to get back to his daily dance routine at "The Golden Age".

In the meantime the fishermen track down the gang. Boris and his friends break into their den. The opposing sides come to blows.

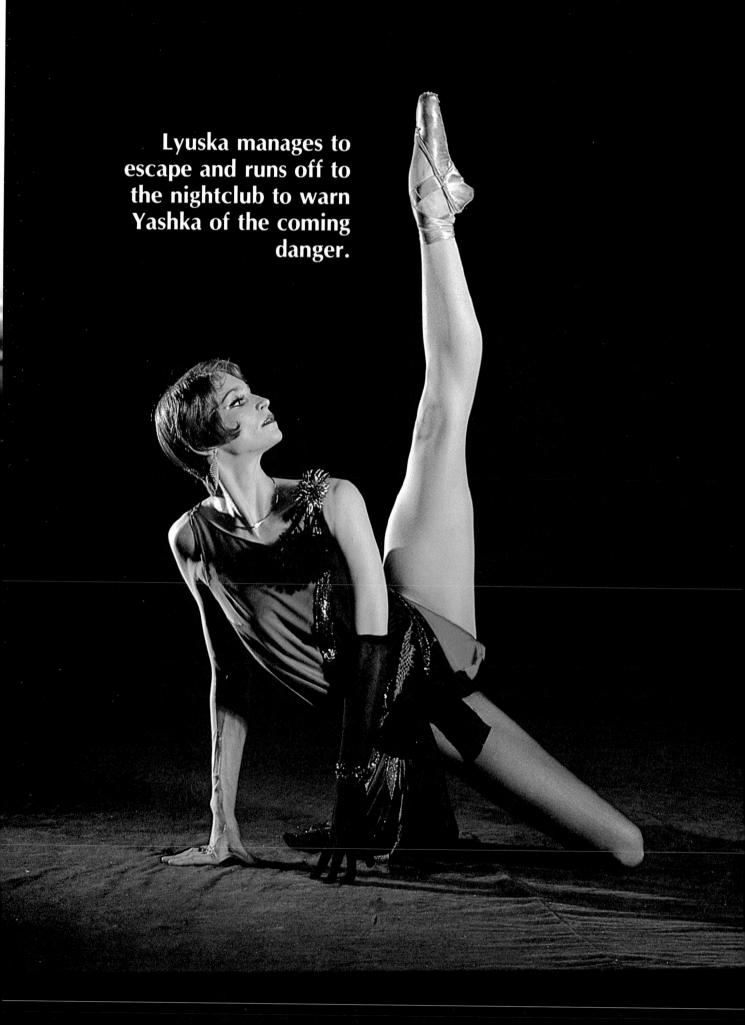

Lyuska manages to escape and runs off to the nightclub to warn Yashka of the coming danger.

The clients of "The Golden Age" ecstatically make merry, unsuspecting the dramatic events taking place in the secret backstage rooms of the restaurant.

Rita and Monsieur Jacques, the favorites of "The Golden Age" clientele, are doing their dancing turn one more time.

Rita is resolute never again to return to the cabaret. For the very last time she performs her famous number—an exotic tango with Monsieur Jacques.

Yashka does not yet know that Rita is firmly resolved to break with her past life and quit the variety club. For her love of Boris she wants to start her life anew. Yashka is still sure Rita will be his...

Lyuska, who is in love with the ringleader, watches him closely. Seeing Yashka seeking Rita's affections makes her blind with rage. She hurls herself at him threatening him and Rita with a knife. And she herself perishes in a violent scene of envy, as in the heat of the struggle Yashka unintentionally stabs her with the same knife.

Rita witnesses Lyuska's death. Now that she knows who her dancing partner really is, she is a serious threat to the gang. In no circumstances can she be allowed to escape. At knife-point Rita is forced by Yashka to go back out onto the stage and do the Apache routine: four men armed with knives follow the defenseless girl. The intoxicated audience does not take earnestly the danseuse's cry for help, thinking it to be part of the acting to make the nerves tingle. They applaud rapturously as Rita is being dragged behind the wings.

The fishermen burst into the restaurant just in time to see Monsieur Jacques making his bows. However, they do not suspect who he really is, thus letting him escape.

The clientele of "The Golden Age" are astounded that the fishermen could be looking for criminals in their favorite entertainment spot. This creates panic among the customers and the performers alike.

Yashka makes a run for his life with those of his hoodlums who are still on the loose. Rita is taken by him as a hostage, but Boris and his friends capture the gangsters and free her.

Rita's nightmare is over. The gang has been broken up. Rita and Boris are together again. They affirm love as the infinite source of life.

Finding herself among the common working people, Rita, a former flamboyant prima donna of a cabaret, is enchanted by the captivating purity of life, its brilliance and boundless horizons.

It is youth, vitality and romantic audacity that triumphs with its deep human aspirations for love, happinesss, and constructive deeds.

Curtain calls for "The Golden Age" at the Bolshoi in Moscow. In the center is Yuri Grigorovich.

A Youth Festivity. Life races on, promising happiness and fulfilment of all good dreams amd desires.

JSC Willey Library
337 College Hill
Johnson, VT 05656

THE GOLDEN AGE

A three-act ballet